CAN THESE BONES LIVE?

Other books of poetry by
ERNEST SANDEEN

A Later Day, Another Year
Collected Poems, 1953–1977
Like Any Road Anywhere
Children and Older Strangers
Antennas of Silence

CAN THESE BONES LIVE?
new poems by

Ernest Sandeen

Foreword by Robert Pinsky
Illustrations by Douglas Kinsey

UNIVERSITY OF NOTRE DAME PRESS
NOTRE DAME, INDIANA

Copyright © 1994 by
Universty of Notre Dame Press
Notre Dame, Indiana 46556

Manufactured in the United States of America

The author is grateful to *Poetry* magazine for permission to reprint "A Late Twentieth-Century Prayer" and "Soon after Nightfall," to *Arts Indiana* for "After Fifty-Seven Years Together," and to *America* for "Old Man Lighting His Pipe."

Library of Congress Cataloging-in-Publication Data

Sandeen, Ernest Emanuel, 1908–
    Can these bones live? : new poems / by Ernest Sandeen.
    p. cm.
    ISBN 0-268-00808-6 (alk. paper)
    1. Aged men—Poetry. I. Title.
PS3537.A6233C36 1994
811'.52—dc20   94-25943
                                                CIP

∞ *The paper used in this publication meets the minimum requirements of the American National Standard for Information Sciences—Permanence of Paper for Printed Library Materials, ANSI Z39.48-1984.*

I wish to dedicate this book to my wife, Eileen, and to my friends, Joan, John, Julie, Max, Sonia and Will. Without their help, this book may never have been completed.

Contents

Foreword *Robert Pinsky*	ix
A Late Twentieth-Century Prayer	1
The Story Lost in Words	2
Surreal and Real	3
First Day, or What You Will	4
A Still Noise	5
When I got out of bed this morning	6
I must have become a ghost haunting	7
A Blip on the Magnified Computer Picture	8
In this once country graveyard	9
Don't spend too much grief	10
College Yearbook, 1931	11
Close your wings, bright angel!	12
September Afternoon	13
Jack and the Beanstalk	14
Can These Bones Live?	15
Old Man Lighting His Pipe	16
Memorial Day	17
Christmas, Year after Year	18
Impasse	19
When I woke up this morning	20
A Summer Solstice Long before Now	21
Trickle Up?	22
His Local Habitation without a Name	23
A Brief Story of Time, Outside and In	24

July 4, 1991	25
An Arbor Day Anniversary	26
At night it is her dreams	27
Mother's Day Greeting	28
After Fifty-Seven Years Together	29
An Affair	30
The Scandal of the Rainbows	31
Early Resources	32
At the Beach	33
A Stranger, Coming and Going	34
Episode: July, 1920	35
Rites of Passage	36
How History Is Made	37
The Gloomy Corner	38
Must I ask of every terror	39
Waiting for a Twitch of Prophesy	40
Aristotle in December	41
Higher Mathematics	42
Any Questions?	43
Now after eighty years of life	44
Last Chance	45
If, after eight-four years, you run out	46
Soon after Nightfall	47
The Spell	48
A fool of the late autumn night	49
Let me assume some far-off	50
Birthday	51
Since I've lost some of the hungers	52
Now I Lay Me	53
How humble our history is!	54
Final Exam	55
Quiz Show	56
Twilight	57
"Do Not Go Gentle"	59

Foreword

The poems of Ernest Sandeen among other things record not only a writing life but a life *in writing*: a history of the hours when reflection turns to discovery, and observation finds its fulfillment in the rhythms of a sentence, the weaving of consonants through a line, in pursuit of a mystery. Few poets have been blessed with the gift to sustain that process of meditation, composing and questioning so consistently, and for so long, in works that are clear and clear-eyed, passionate and precise.

So it is with renewed wonder that readers can see the poet in his most recent poems regarding all that various, wide terrain, with gaze as clear as ever and still allured by the mystery, not flinching from it:

A STILL NOISE

There once occurred a silence,
all dark and odorless, that commanded me
to halt and listen. How could I refuse?
And now after so many years ago

how can I remember what I heard?
I have waited too long: the dead
have become too many and too explicit,
and the living suspect nothing.

Much of the well-measured poetry of this poem hinges on the tough, perhaps startling word "explicit": the literal, exacting reality of those dead, like letters spelling a sentence the cloudy, unknowing living cannot read.

Explicitness that acknowledges mystery: that would be one way to define the virtues of Sandeen's writing. In "A Brief Story of Time, Outside and In" the explicit presents itself as a series of sounds, and the great mystery is embodied in what those sounds add up to for the perceiver:

> What he hears first is the unceasing, merciless din of
>   traffic
> along the nearby highway punctuated
> with dissenting sirens. And then from across the river
>
> he detects the church tower keeping the faith,
> storing each hour away, melodious quarter by quarter.
> What is left for him to do is to listen for silences
>
> within himself deep enough to resonate into one
> inexpressible meaning the fury of the pavement
> with the meditative bell.

Meaning, even inexpressible meaning is the object of the poet's quest, and the poems have the confident wisdom to locate their grail in silence. In the poem "Soon after Nightfall," where the murmured, uncomprehended words of a prayer are called "the wisdom of the Elders," that phrase is earned.

It is easy enough to invoke the names of silence and mystery; in this career they convince, because they are rooted in the daily noises of traffic and the wails of ordinary calamity. In this collection, nuggets and small, bright fragments of poetry find a place—held among those deep-going roots, the nourishing, soil-fed tangle that feeds the green crown.

Robert Pinsky

CAN THESE BONES LIVE?

A Late Twentieth-Century Prayer

We've been taught for two thousand years
that not a single sparrow can fall
outside your notice. And now
you've given us leave to perfect

microscopic spectacles insightful enough
to show us your meticulous concern
with these minute particles in the body
of the world we inhabit, so alien to our everyday

perception we know them only by their nicknames,
some of them snuffed out in fractions of a second.
You must have, then, some inclination
to attend to all my little kind and me,

orphaned on earth, this tiny cinder flung
helplessly around and around
a helplessly burning star. We trust your interest
in us may be what locally we call love.

The Story Lost in Words

One midwinter morning he finds
that he has lost his ancestral Bible.
Hours later in the dusk of twilight
he's sure he has uncovered it
from under his pile of disheveled newspapers.

But his study-lamp reveals his error:
the book under his thumb is a dictionary.

It's as if the whole law and the prophets,
Pentateuch and Gospels, have crumbled
into bits and pieces, mere words arranged
in a mad, meaningless alphabetical order.

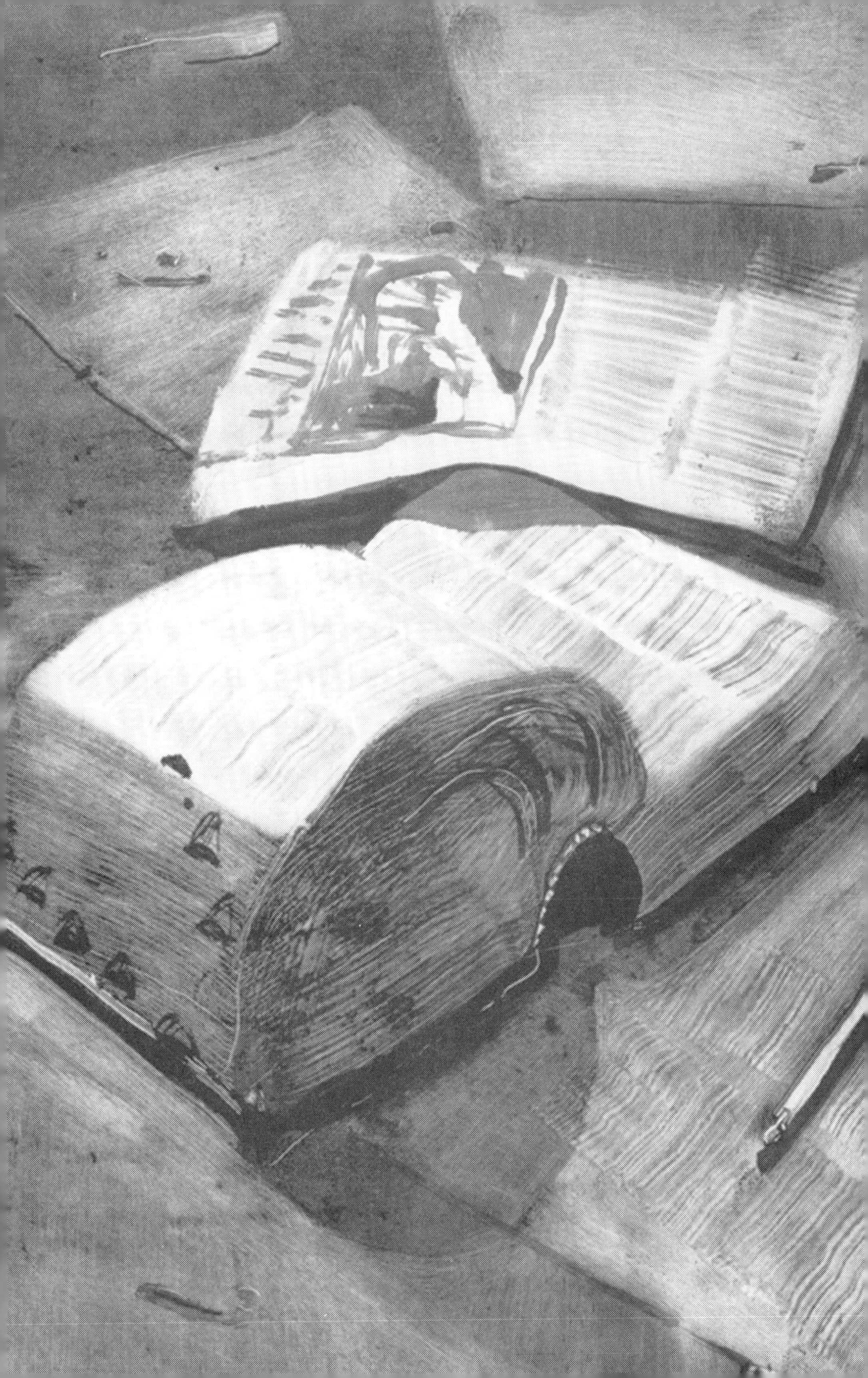

Surreal and Real

Although you were barely prompt enough,
you did glimpse time blending into space
in Einstein's brain. But luckily you
didn't throw your watch away;
because it's Newton who has remained your closest friend
and neighbor.

First Day, or What You Will

He thinks there must have been an unplanned
micro-delay in the big explosion which launched
existence into space. That explains, he says

why everything since then is slightly time-
flawed, happening a little too late (or sometimes
too soon which is too late turned inside out).

A Still Noise

There once occurred a silence,
all dark and odorless, that commanded me
to halt and listen. How could I refuse?
And now after so many years ago

how can I remember what I heard?
I have waited too long: the dead
have become too many and too explicit,
and the living suspect nothing.

When I Got Out of Bed This Morning

When I got out of bed this morning
to join our human tribe, it felt as if
we were all moving together through
our calender-defined parade of days.

Until I felt someone stepping on
my heels. I thought it must be
a stranger. But looking back
I understood how he didn't even

see me. How could he? He was
myself of sixty years ago
when I was living forever every day.

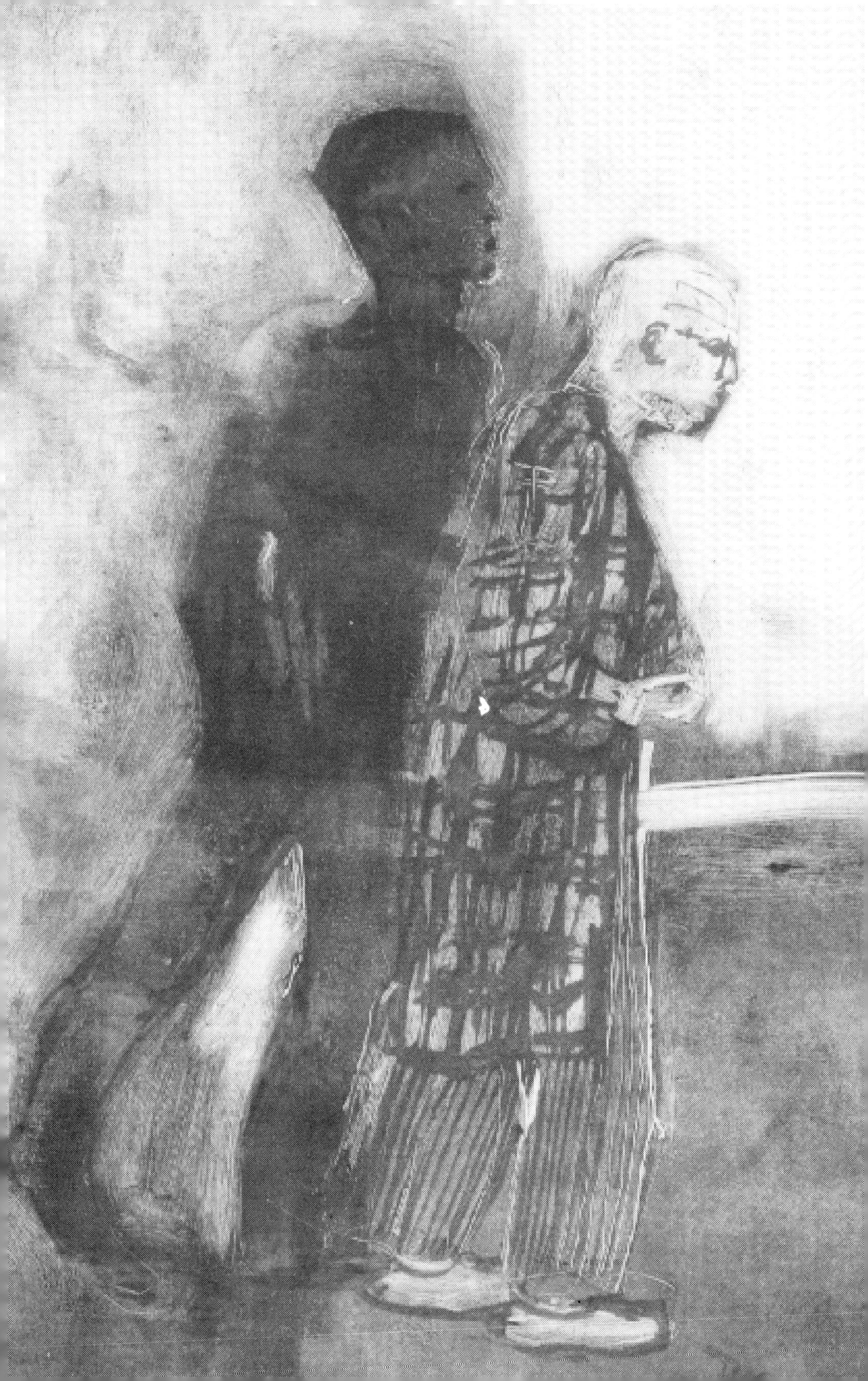

I MUST HAVE BECOME
A GHOST HAUNTING

I must have become a ghost haunting
the several lives I've outlived, a disguise
to protect me for a time from that identity
which is as fatal as history.

A Blip on the Magnified Computer Picture

On your way to the barbershop
you're almost blown off your feet
when it occurs to you that you're
using some of the very same time
needed to keep the galaxies
spinning through the light-years.

In this once country graveyard

In this once country graveyard,
now caught in the tentacles
of a noisily expanding city,
we can feel more intimately than ever
the heavy demands made upon us
by the dead. Here they stand
idling, day and night in the din
of traffic, as mute as time
itself, as still as stone.

They require nothing less
of us than our lives.

Don't spend too much grief

Don't spend too much grief
on burial grounds and their inhabitants.
Save some for yourself. It's a good investment.
Already you begin to see satisfying results
for everything that lives,
for everything that dies.

College Yearbook, 1931

How can we forget how eager
these professors were to disturb
our young, unexamined lives
with their own ardent doubts and beliefs?

And now here they lie as if
snugly tucked into their graves.
Did they find no further place
to go than here into our mortal memories?

Close your wings, bright angel!

Close your wings, bright angel!
They expose me to light which I have
not as yet learned either to absorb
or avoid. It only threatens me,
do you understand? And it hurts.

September Afternoon

Crisp wings of butterflies are creating out of
nothing but air, caverns of fish
pregnant with the mind of eagles.

Can we imagine that some strolling dream
of ours as dull as sleep itself stubbed its toe
on a nub of nothing at all and exploded
us into where we are now, looking around
                and wondering?

Jack and the Beanstalk

I've tried to pry myself upward
with extravagant prayers
but as I near my last days (and nights)
I discover I've reached only the rooftop of the house
I've lived in all my life.

And to tell the truth
I really can't see much more from here
than I saw from some of the more
modest elevations below.

"Can These Bones Live?"
Ezekiel 37:3

From the clock I've always lived in the presence of
but have never seen I sense a warning
more intimate than touch that I am nearing
the event which is as desperate as birth.

Small wonder, then, that I have misgivings.
For instance, I've never been taught how to crawl
out of a human skeleton decorously and with skill.

If only I could remember how I managed
to infiltrate this nest of bones
in the first place—
but I can't.

Old Man Lighting His Pipe

Once a year you smoke your pipe
in season; we call it Indian summer.

Tobacco, the Indians' gift to the white man
to rot his lungs and forked tongue,
a delayed revenge for the paleface
gift of rot-gut firewater and firearms.

You imagine those Chiefs of the Indian Nations
seated in a solemn ring, passing the pipe,
one to the other, their news of peace rising
enlarged, in smoke signals, from hill to hill.

Now you see smokestacks and the exhaust
pipes from miles of traffic sending up
diffused, unreadable signals, city to city.

Children, no longer amused by the smoke
rings you can blow, are blowing bubbles,
galaxies of spheres, shining, floating
with no need of fire, on air as still as peace,
then exploding noiselessly on the green lawn.

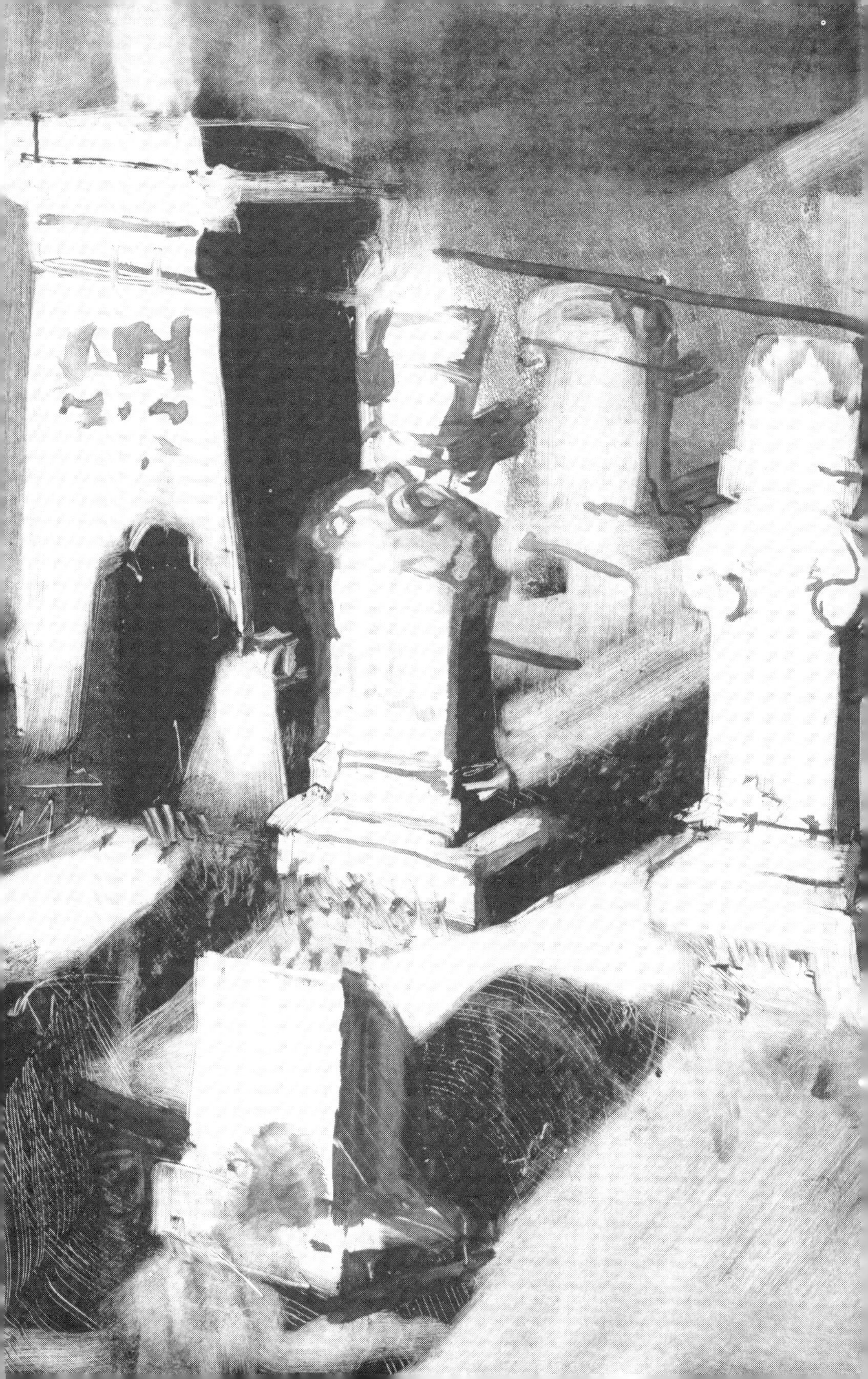

Memorial Day

On this day every year
our dead afflict us with
a kind of solemn astonishment
at how close to us they remain.

The dates on their headstones
reveal that even in their graves
they grow older year by year
just as we do. They are still with us.
We are all going in the same direction.

Christmas, Year after Year

On this day which we proclaim God
has made we forgive the poor for being
always with us. We pardon them
with baskets of groceries, bundles of used
blankets, outgrown coats and boots.

We recreate them in our own
image for this one day, making
them warm, well shod and well fed like us.

Impasse

His fourth-grade teacher shouted
at him (in class) "Answer me!"
He knew she meant to say, "Anchor
me!" because she had been
floundering in deep water for some
time, maybe all her life. His
hair stood up on end because
he was only a small boy not strong
enough or smart enough to rescue her.

When I Woke Up This Morning

When I woke up this morning, I counted my fingers
to test those bewildering, repetitious dreams
of the night. There were still five digits on each hand
including the two opposing thumbs needed
for grasping things, sometimes so intimately
that things feel as naked as nothing but thoughts.

I wonder, could the tail I abandoned millions
of years ago have gotten itself reconstructed
into that invisible, prehensile thing
I swing around on inside my head?

A Summer Solstice Long before Now

It cost you only the expense
of a single puckish summer night
to discover that elves, pixies,
or even old-fashioned angels
can't lead your life for you.

They are too inexperienced.

The most they can do is exclaim
in amazement at your follies,
then gasp in wonder at how
you manage to escape, your life intact.

Trickle Up?

Does human evolution have a future?
Even our dog is troubled by the limited
significance of our presence. He whines
at the door wanting to get out.

His Local Habitation without a Name

When we found him drinking our furniture polish
he explained quite simply he had run out of beer.
It was not so much the taste which exhilarated
him, he admitted, as it was the ruddy harvest
color. And finally there were those words printed
on the label like a rubric, "An end to dust."
And wasn't it dust he would soon need
to be delivered from?

A Brief Story of Time, Outside and In

When he comes face to face with the kitchen clock,
he crosses himself because he's old enough to know that early
or late it's time that threatens him.

And now he can sit and listen to the night outside.

What he hears first is the unceasing, merciless din of traffic
along the nearby highway punctuated
with dissenting sirens. And then from across the river

he detects the church tower keeping the faith,
storing each hour away, melodious quarter by quarter.
What is left for him to do is to listen for silences

within himself deep enough to resonate into one
inexpressible meaning the fury of the pavement
with the meditative bell.

July 4, 1991

Please don't inflict your flag
on my defenseless body. I have
an old horse blanket that
keeps my blood warm on the
coldest nights. The horse himself
galloped away some years ago.

An Arbor Day Anniversary

The tulip tree lifts its flowers up
like a host of candles to be
lighted by the infinite blue sky,

and we can feel our earthly afternoon
come alive with blessings
in every tingling pore and cell.

At night it is her dreams

At night it is her dreams
that drive her silently
across the vast fantastic
regions of her sleep.

and when she wakes
she finds that they've
returned her to her bed,
her pillow scarcely ruffled.

She wonders if there could be
a morning when her dreams
might lose their way and fail
to bring her back again.

At what outlandish place
might she be then forever stranded.

MOTHER'S DAY GREETING

My longtime lover and wife, receive
this gentle May-morning rain as if
it were my gift to you on the day which
our public calendar decrees is yours.

Only you and I know that my feigned gift
of rain means our grateful loss of the
many long dry seasons which we had
to endure before these beautiful new

people consented to appear and
complete our lives with theirs.

After Fifty-Seven Years Together

We can only wonder how lightly
we have left behind, one by one,
the different love affairs we have had
with one another.

                    During this pause
before all memories fade, by merely
touching hands we can celebrate
our loyal infidelities to those
passing lovers we once were,

now most precious to us but then,
each pair in turn, threatening to become
as fixed as the end of time.

An Affair

It's the light of a full moon that invades
her sleep but her dream persuades her
it must be bird or bat, her bed
being so near roof and rafters.

It's a soft terror that holds her,
downy and feathery, a prolonged
near ecstasy like a frustrated
orgasm. It leaves her pounding
a velvet door which conceals
nothing but the silence of light-years.

When she wakens, all she remembers
is secretly holding hands
with the foamy pale water
of the fountain in the city square.

The Scandal of the Rainbows

At the foot of this morning's rainbow
we found no pot of gold, only
a pat of butter waiting
for our late breakfast.

Of course, after such a long
history as ours of eons
spent in darkness, we
have learned to expect

our days to emerge more
modestly into light than those
father Adam named into being
and Uncle Noah, ages later,
had to rescue from a mountain top.

Early Resources

I still remember when my body
and I were playmates, perfect
equals, head to toe. While still
crawling we shared secrets which we

kept strictly to ourselves as
the gentle unsuspecting giants
went on crooning over us.

At the Beach

When she saw the naked imprint
of his big toe in the wet sand,
she wondered if it was an indicator
of his physical endowment.

All the next day it filled her
with the most pleasing surmises.

Gave her a toe-hold, you might say.

A Stranger, Coming and Going

She has a face
too sweetly innocent
to give fair warning
of a derriere
so provocative.

Episode: July, 1920

One summer afternoon when he was
twelve and his parents had left him
alone in the house, he stripped off
all his clothes, crept out the back door
and raced down the brick sidewalk
to the family privy at the lower end of the yard.

And waiting there in the half-light
were those grown women in the slick pages
of the Sears and Roebuck catalogue,
dressed only in tightly fitting underwear.
They kept on smiling straight at him
even when he showed them how
completely naked he was, all over.
Why did it please him to know
that they could never be friends of his mother?

But what did they really want of him?
He lingered with them as long as he dared
enjoying more and more the danger
he was in of being caught without his clothes.
After his panicky flight back to the house
he was trembling and breathing hard.
It was then he got scared. For the very
reason that he had nothing he could tell them
he wished mother and father would get home soon.

Rites of Passage

The girl bass-drummer in the high school band
banged out the punctuation of the Sousa march
with such fierce emphasis he felt exposed
as if she had shattered the playpen
where his mother had put him fifteen years before.

And when she crashed those cymbals together
he was ready to fall at her feet and plead for mercy.

How could she do it, her face so sweetly gentle,
her slender figure so lightly graceful?
He had to know, he had to see her alone,
perhaps in a private booth at Pearl's
Ice Cream Parlor. But how could he ever ask her?

What if she might accept?

How History Is Made

"My God!" cried the Princess, "take your hand
off my knee!" And she was right, of course.
Because it was history they were in, after all,

and if his twiddling fingers had been
permitted to go on exploring the enticements
of her more intimate clefts and protrusions
who knows what might have happened
to all the arrangements the future
had already made for later memorable
battlefields and famous speeches printed
for schoolbooks growing children might
memorize and recite for generation after generation.

The Gloomy Corner

is formed out of a deep basic
weariness below the level of sunlight,
yet "dark" is too innocent a word
to name it. The slight tinge of guilty
involvement hinted at in "gloomy" is needed.

This structure of elusive intangibles
is best built during an afternoon just
bright enough for the gloom to show through.

A room inside a room is as old
as your childhood when you threw
a blanket over the backs of two chairs
opposite each other and then crawled
into the cave you had made. You felt
oddly at home, strangely secure.
You were already too old to remember the womb.

The gloomy room has a couch but no bed.
It's a place of rest you've spent your life
creating. It's not a marble slab in a morgue
nor the tousled sheets of wild pleasure;
only a gentle place of disciplined dozing.

Must I ask of every terror

Must I ask of every terror
that assaults my sleep:
are you from hell or from heaven
in disguise? What is it

comes out of the dark
to wound my private sorrow?
Is nothing sacred?

Waiting for a Twitch of Prophesy

It's only a light-switch away.
But it's still dark, very dark,
my friends. I have to sleep
in order to remember your names.
Strategies like heart-beat
and breathing are involved.
I hope you understand.

Aristotle in December

I feel special pangs of pity and fear
for those called upon to die in winter.
It seems a reckless, brutal addition
to the fate of all the rest of us
deeply doomed enough already.

Higher Mathematics

The benefit of living beyond eighty
is that bone marrow and every nerve end
begin to tell you that all your decades
however many will add up at the end
to total loss.

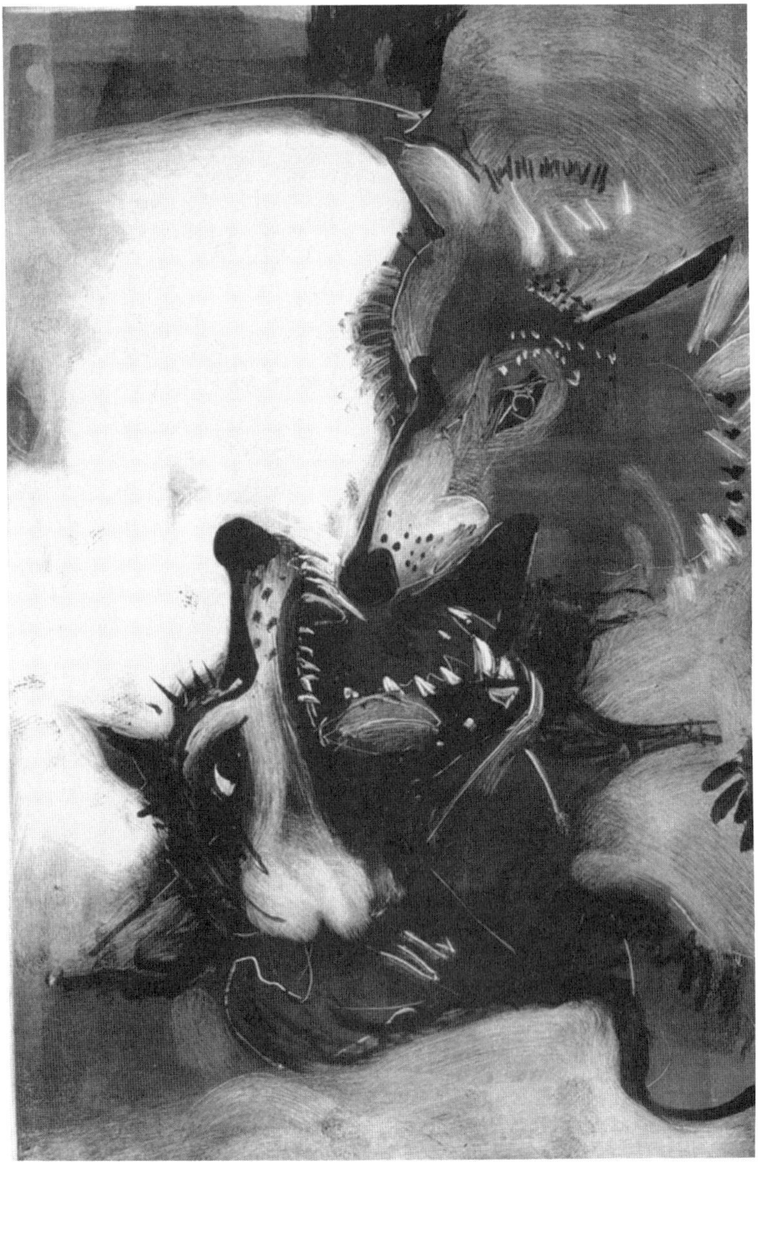

Any Questions?

While trying for over eighty years
to become real have I been learning
nothing but nomenclature? that wife,
children, friends are only nominal?

Be careful, old man; such impolitic
queries come close to the quick, can
draw blood. Just below the skin
lives an animal whose deft pretense

to honor your grammar may turn
to treasonous, dangerous deviations.
What you hear along the sidelines
are hounds howling, tomcats screaming,

donkeys braying. Are *these* the answers
to the questions your years
have kept on asking and asking?

Now After Eighty Years of Life

Now after eighty years of life
I discover that all
I have wanted to do
was to write a poem that would love me,
all the way through my pretenses
but without pampering me
like the spoiled child I suspect I am.

Yet how hard it is to accept gifts,
especially when they prove to be necessities,

like friends and lovers
and enemies and death also
even though too stupid
to do or say or feel
or think anything at all.

Last Chance

Each spring for eighty-two years
you have survived the brutal
green and flowering onslaught
of new life in everything around you,
from the humble grass to the tallest treetops.

And still you stumble around in the same
stupor of ignorance you were born with.

You're approaching what may be
your last chance. If the violence
of death, attacking you in every
cell of your body, can't wake you up,
what in Heaven's name can?

IF, AFTER EIGHTY-FOUR YEARS, YOU RUN OUT

If, after eighty-four years, you run out
of faith, don't give up hope
which may prove to be the only
real resource you've ever had.

In fact, it may be hope as naked
of tint or color as the air itself
which alone can smuggle
you into your remaining years,

and, who knows, may even ease you
with all the innocence of love into that vacancy
beyond time which we have never learned
to measure, not its beginning and not its end.

Soon after Nightfall

Watch the old codger toddle off
to bed and to his lullaby prayers
which he has no more need to understand
now than when he first heard
his mother murmuring them.
It's the wisdom of the Elders
descending from generation to generation.

The Spell

Watching night come on after
a whole day of steady snowfall
is a story of someone dying
all your life long among white sheets.

You could nudge yourself
to make sure it's not you
but you know there's no need.

A FOOL OF THE LATE AUTUMN NIGHT

A fool of the late autumn night
he stumbles indoors, slamming the screen
behind him, his hair full of cold
rain, his head full of clouds
whose end and meaning
he knows he will not have time to decipher.

Let Me Assume Some Far-Off

Let me assume some far-off,
long-ago space in time where
I met inadvertently a creature-song
as inescapable and persistent
as destiny. It was music I am
only now beginning to hear
although I must have been humming it
to myself all my eighty-five years.

BIRTHDAY

Imagine the hubbub
among all the people,
some not yet even imagined,
when he announces,
"I'm going to be born
tomorrow!"

A few cry out, "Already?"
Others warn, "You'll be too early!"
"Or most likely too late,"
mutter the elders, losing
interest, already dozing.

Since I've lost some
of the hungers I once

Since I've lost some of the hungers I once
needed to survive, beautiful fish come
cavorting into my easy sleep merely
to amuse and entertain me along the way.

Now I Lay Me

On my way to bed
I whisper to the clock
on the mantel (or wink)
Because I'm hoping the air
between us, being deaf
and blind will soon let me
dwindle softly into the warm
timeless nowhere of sleep
(without, of course, letting
me blunder into spaces
too far and deep to waken from).

How humble our history is!

How humble our history is!
a long line of ancestors unknowingly
growing these heads we wear
from the bloody paths traced
by their tails.

Final Exam

Was this what we were meant to grow into
through those millions of years—
creatures that can name all things
around them and so build a second
creation out of nothing but sounds
in their throats and mouths? Has Adam

then (our old namer), actually identified
nothing, being only a doll
on an unknown ventriloquist's knee?

Quiz Show

Small children can ask you
without words, simply by staring
at everything around them including
you: All right, we're here. What
happened? Where do we go?

Thirty years later they're
saying with an excess of words
and gestures (sometimes violent):
All right. We're still here. What's
next? The best answer you can

give from what you've learned
in three decades is this: it's
childhood all over again but with
a difference: the meanings get simpler,
the words get harder to find.

TWILIGHT

A pair of spectacles and a pair
of hearing aids are at rest
on the dining room table like dice
in the posture of a loss we can't interpret.

We know that all the clues we once thought
we had are aging into a second ignorance,
though not as innocent as the first.

What we long for now is a simple
miracle. Not a heroic deed of the mind
but a brute bodily fact as for instance:
"One thing I know: I was blind and now I see."

At last we have learned that time
is always relentlessly modern.
The heaven that the angels sang
has melted back into common stars.

Was the hound of rescue, then,
that pursued us down the years
only the sound of our own hard breathing?

Our long parade of years is drenched
in silent farewells performed under dripping
graveside umbrellas. Mud it was,
but still we said, dust to dust, with one hand.

Is that sound you hear only
an inquisitive wind in the eaves
or the mutter of prayer wheels and beads?

Gentle lies are being told under the hill
almost in whispers. No harm is meant.
Twilight is beginning or ending
something as accidental as a seed
dropped from the beak of a bird
returning to its nest at nightfall.

There's an emptiness widening
in the weather and a mild wind
pressing us as close to nothing
as we can get without dissolving.

But only at the absolute, soundless
end may we hope to learn that
there is no end, that whatever
else he may be, God is no atheist.